BRIAN JOHNSTON

Can You Profess Christ and Still Be Lost?

Contents

1

Law and Grace: Two Different Freedoms

Ever since the Apostle Paul wrote the words: *"you are not under law but under grace"* (Romans 6:14 RV), the debate has never ended. It once became particularly controversial in 18th century Scotland over the publication of a book with the now strange sounding title of *The Marrow of Modern Divinity.* As with bone marrow, its title was hinting at its attempt to get to the core of the Gospel. But what exactly is the debate?

In the Christian life, even among genuine believers, some will tend toward legalistic thinking. Even though they know their acceptance before God is not based on their performance, they still tend to live their lives in that way and perhaps judge others on the same basis. On the other hand, some other genuine Christians get taken up with the idea of the freedom of grace. They think they can live as they please, even becoming careless about avoiding sinful practices.

If we look at the Bible truths that Paul was teaching on around that key verse in Romans 6:14, we could describe the ongoing

1

debate as being about getting a true understanding of, on the one hand, what the Bible calls 'Justification' and, on the other hand, what the Bible calls 'Sanctification.' We should make it clear what these specialist Bible words mean. To 'justify' means to declare someone righteous, certainly meaning they're not guilty. And to 'sanctify' means to set someone or something apart, as devoted for some special use for someone. It would often come to include the idea of being holy, in the sense of being different from or set apart from what's profane. Difficulties can arise if we use the word 'salvation' to mean, in effect, both to be declared as not guilty before God and to be set apart as holy. When we do that, we've sacrificed some accuracy and this can sadly lead to serious confusion.

The reason is the Bible is emphatic that we're justified by God's grace alone. The Bible explicitly says we're justified as a gift by God's grace (Romans 3:24). That's grace, meaning God's undeserved favour towards us; not based on any merit whatsoever on our part. But the Bible is also equally emphatic that we're to become in daily living what we are in God's sight. We're to 'become what we already are' in the sense that we've been declared holy but now we need to display holiness. Paul opens his first letter to the local Church of God at Corinth by telling them they were holy (ones) by God's calling (1 Corinthians 1:2). Soon, however, by the time we get to the third chapter, we find him correcting their carnal behaviours (1 Corinthians 3:3). As Peter told his readers, they needed to be holy as God is holy (1 Peter 1:15,16).

What we're saying is this: for us to be justified or declared righteous in God's sight is totally God's work. We don't and can't contribute anything to that. But, there's an ongoing aspect to being sanctified in daily life that actively requires our co-operation with the Spirit of God who lives inside every true believer on the Lord Jesus. The result is that if we talk about our being saved without clarifying exactly what we mean by that – whether being justified or being sanctified – it can be like talking about apples and oranges: that is, two different things.

Let's now bring the debate back to the terms of law and grace that we were reading about in Romans 6:14, where it says we're no longer under law but under grace. When we use 'salvation' to mean 'justification' – and leave 'sanctification' out of the discussion, it can seem as if we're hinting that a sort of lawless or careless type of living (sometimes labelled as 'antinomianism') is somehow acceptable, or at least tolerable. But if we should use 'salvation' to mean 'sanctification' – and leave 'justification' out of the discussion, someone is likely to yell 'legalism!' because they, on their part, are thinking salvation is all about justification whereas they think we're stressing our performance. It really would be more helpful if we always made absolutely clear when we're talking about the means of our salvation (justified by grace through faith alone), and not about our response to salvation (co-operating with the Spirit in ongoing sanctification).

When we truly receive Christ as our personal saviour and live by remaining in God's love, then we're freed from the necessity of having to perform in a certain way, but we're also freed to do the specific good works that he's planned for us (see Ephesians 2:8–10). Those are two different freedoms. The dispensation of Law was not without grace; and the dispensation or age of Grace is not anti-law.

In terms of Jesus' Parable of the Prodigal Son, we could view the elder brother as legalistic and the prodigal as antinomian (from anti- meaning against and nomian meaning law). This means the younger or prodigal son may be viewed as anti-law or careless, even lawless in his behaviour. Both sons needed to come to their father, who stood ready to extend grace and enjoy their fellowship. Perhaps it would be worth unpacking that a bit more, for we often, I suspect, see this story as having a one-time application in our lives relating to the 'before' and 'after' of our testimony of how we came to Christ. The thing that ought to be plain to us from the timing and setting of where we read this story in the Bible is who the main characters in the story represent. Let's remind ourselves of what was happening: "*Now all the tax collectors and sinners were coming near Jesus to listen to Him. And both the Pharisees and the scribes began to complain, saying, "This man receives sinners and eats with them*" (Luke 15:1-2). Not long after that, we read:

> "*And He [Jesus] said, 'A man had two sons. The younger of them said to his father, 'Father, give me the share of the estate that is coming to me.' And so he divided his wealth between them. And not many days later, the younger son gathered everything together and went on a journey to a distant country, and there he squandered his estate in wild living. Now when he had spent everything, a severe famine occurred in that country, and he began doing without. So he went and hired himself out to one of the citizens of that country, and he sent him into his fields to feed pigs. And he longed to have his fill of the carob*

pods that the pigs were eating, and no one was giving him anything.

But when he came to his senses, he said, 'How many of my father's hired laborers have more than enough bread, but I am dying here from hunger! I will set out and go to my father, and will say to him, "Father, I have sinned against heaven, and in your sight; I am no longer worthy to be called your son; treat me as one of your hired laborers."' So he set out and came to his father. But when he was still a long way off, his father saw him and felt compassion for him, and ran and embraced him and kissed him. And the son said to him, 'Father, I have sinned against heaven and in your sight; I am no longer worthy to be called your son.' But the father said to his slaves, 'Quickly bring out the best robe and put it on him, and put a ring on his finger and sandals on his feet; and bring the fattened calf, slaughter it, and let's eat and celebrate; for this son of mine was dead and has come to life again; he was lost and has been found.' And they began to celebrate.

"Now his older son was in the field, and when he came and approached the house, he heard music and dancing. And he summoned one of the servants and began inquiring what these things could be. And he said to him, 'Your brother has come, and your father has slaughtered the fattened calf because he has received him back safe and sound.' But he became angry and was not willing to go in; and his father came out and began pleading with him. But he answered and said to his father, 'Look! For so many years I have been serving you and I have never

neglected a command of yours; and yet you never gave me a young goat, so that I might celebrate with my friends; but when this son of yours came, who has devoured your wealth with prostitutes, you slaughtered the fattened calf for him.' And he said to him, 'Son, you have always been with me, and all that is mine is yours. But we had to celebrate and rejoice, because this brother of yours was dead and has begun to live, and was lost and has been found.'" (Luke 15:11-32).

Plainly, the reference points are these: the prodigal is designed to make us think in terms of the tax collectors and other blatant sinners with whom Jesus was accused of fraternising. And, by way of contrast, the elder brother seems to be pointing at the Pharisees and scribes, the party who were doing the accusing.

The younger, prodigal, brother lived very carelessly; he was in fact a 'loose-liver.' He depicts the person who lives in a lawless or antinomian way. We're familiar with the fact that when he came to his senses, he was warmly received by his father. His stay-at-home older brother illustrates the legalist who claims never to have broken any laws or commands. There's a self-righteousness about him, a smugness perhaps, that's less appealing. But let's remember that Saul of Tarsus was a leading Pharisee who came to Christ. Nicodemus and Joseph of Arimathea also came out from the shadows and made public their allegiance to Christ. Have we been too hasty to write off the elder brother in this parable? After all, the father said to him: '... you have been always with me, and all that is mine is yours.' The point I'm making is this: that in the ranks of lawless 'antinomians' and also among the ranks of legalists, there are genuine Christians to be found.

What we need to learn is this: that we're freed from the charges of God's Law that were against us. That is, we're now **justified**, and that's all of God. At the same time, however, we're enslaved to the God of the Law. That is, we're being **sanctified**, and that's something we cooperate with God in doing. We're now free to do what pleases God. It's not intended that we live as we please, but we're meant to realise that our acceptance is not based on our performance.

2

Is It Possible To Be a Carnal Christian?

We're told there are three kinds of people in the world. Anthropologists talk about caucasoid, mongoloid and negroid races. But biblically we're all one human race! The Apostle Paul, in Acts chapter 17, says that God made from one man every nation of humanity (v.26). There's no basis whatsoever for being racist if you take the Bible seriously. There's only one human race and that includes all of us! The Bible, however, might at first glance seem to have a classification scheme of its own. It has been viewed as dividing us into three kinds of people. Let's hear from Paul as we break into First Corinthians chapter 2 and verse 13:

> *"We ... speak these things, not in words taught by human wisdom, but in those taught by the Spirit, combining spiritual thoughts with spiritual words. But a natural person does not accept the things of the Spirit of God, for they are foolishness to him; and he cannot understand them, because they are spiritually discerned. But the one who is spiritual discerns all things, yet he himself*

is discerned by no one. For WHO HAS KNOWN THE MIND OF THE LORD, THAT HE WILL INSTRUCT HIM? But we have the mind of Christ. And I, brothers and sisters, could not speak to you as spiritual people, but only as fleshly, as to infants in Christ. I gave you milk to drink, not solid food; for you were not yet able to consume it. But even now you are not yet able, for you are still fleshly. For since there is jealousy and strife among you, are you not fleshly, and are you not walking like ordinary people?" (1 Corinthians 2:13-3:3).

Perhaps you picked out from that reading what's been suggested as the three types of person? They're people who are natural or else spiritual, but these latter may be also carnal (fleshly, or it may be translated as worldly). To be more definite, if we were to stick to the language this part of the Bible was written in: the words are *psuchikos*, *pneumatikos* and *sarkikos*. Let's take the first of the three - starting with *psuchikos* or 'natural.' This refers to someone born into their natural family and living in a natural way.

Next, we have *pneumatikos* or 'spiritual' types. This refers to someone born again into God's spiritual family and living in a spiritual way. Finally, we come to a potential third category – and here it gets a bit more controversial – for this is *sarkikos* or 'carnal,' and so often taken with the meaning of a worldly Christian. This describes someone born again into God's spiritual family but living in some areas of their life in a natural way.

Why did I say 'controversial' a moment ago? Well, when Paul was asked "What must I do to be saved?" he answered: "Believe on the Lord Jesus and you will be saved" (Acts 16:31). Note the title: Lord Jesus. It's not possible to trust in Christ as Saviour without necessarily confessing Christ as Lord. It's not possible to profess genuine faith without first having repented of sin. We deny that anyone can be saved by their own good works, but equally we affirm the place of good works in the subsequent Christian life of the true believer. The Bible is crystal clear that we're justified not by works, but by faith alone (Galatians 2:16). But it's equally clear that the faith that justifies us is never alone. Any true profession of real faith will show evidence of some works, for obedience springs from faith (see Romans 1:5 & 16:26). If we never see good works in another person, we must at least doubt whether they're really a Christian.

Loving Christ means we obey him (John 14:15). On the other hand, obedience will never be perfect in this lifetime. The presence of sin makes sure of that. But true faith will inevitably result in obedience, however imperfect it may be. True Christians live a life characterized by a war between the Holy Spirit and the flesh (our old sin nature, Romans 7:13−20; Galatians 5:16−24). Sometimes our sinful nature seems to be winning more battles than the Spirit (e.g. 1 Corinthians 3:1−4). This was true of the Apostle Paul himself, as he confesses in Romans 7:15,16, saying he often did things he didn't want to do. It's especially true when we're still spiritual infants. It doesn't mean we're not saved; because the presence of a desire for obedience (such as Paul expressed) and to do good works prove otherwise.

If and when someone has said 'the sinner's prayer' and asked the Lord to save them on one occasion, we must wait to observe fruit before we can be confident to consider them a true and genuine believer in Christ. It's safe to say that it's not possible to be born of the Spirit and for there to be no change whatsoever in one's life.

In his Parable of the Sower (Mark 4:1-20), the Lord illustrated how it would be possible for someone to receive the word and grow spiritually for a while but then become discouraged by difficulties or become entangled in the things of this life that act like thorns, strangling any visible Christian lifestyle. We have to be so careful in our assessments of others.

It would be unwise then or indeed wrong to try to establish this third category of those who are 'carnal' in the same way as the first two categories of those who are natural or spiritual. For that would be to raise the spectre of the old heresy of 'antinomianism.' As we've mentioned, 'Anti' means 'no' or 'against' and 'nomian' means 'law.' In other words, antinomianism is the teaching that a Christian may practice a lawless life without the rule of Christ in his or her heart.

Early in his letter to the Corinthians, Paul rebuked the church for a measure of carnality in their lives. They were acting as unregenerate people in an area of their lives. For as long as there was jealousy and envying, they couldn't be taught the deeper things of the Lord. Yet they weren't altogether without evidence of the Spirit. Paul wasn't saying they were living without *any* spiritual fruit in their lives: in fact, he said in everything they were enriched by Christ—in their words, thoughts and life.

That then begs the question: was Paul saying that the Corinthians' lives were characterized by carnality as a whole? Or were these people with new hearts who were producing authentic spiritual fruit but, as all believers do at times, they were struggling with various areas of their lives, and it was affecting the whole church in this instance?

This may lead us to query if Paul was indeed dividing the people into three classes: natural, spiritual and carnal. If we were to hold to that threefold division in some sense, we'd want to make it quite clear that to style some as carnal is not to say that some Christians may legitimately be characterised as carnal as a whole, only that it's a description of believers who typically and visibly display sinful behaviours – such that it's a prominent feature, sadly. Let's hear again from the Apostle Paul, but this time from that great chapter we know of as Romans chapter 8:

> *"For what the Law could not do, weak as it was through the flesh, God did: sending His own Son in the likeness of sinful flesh and as an offering for sin, He condemned sin in the flesh, so that the requirement of the Law might be fulfilled in us who do not walk according to the flesh but according to the Spirit. For those who are in accord with the flesh set their minds on the things of the flesh, but those who are in accord with the Spirit, the things of the Spirit.*
>
> *For the mind set on the flesh is death, but the mind set on the Spirit is life and peace, because the mind set on the flesh is hostile toward God; for it does not subject itself to the law of God, for it is not even able to do so, and those who are in the flesh cannot please God. However, you are not in the flesh but in the Spirit, if indeed the Spirit of God*

dwells in you. But if anyone does not have the Spirit of Christ, he does not belong to Him" (Romans 8:3-9).

We can here identify the same three categories of people: first, those who are in the flesh; second, those who are in the Spirit and living in accordance with the Spirit; and third, those who are in the Spirit but typically living in accord with the flesh. In other words, those who are in the flesh are natural or unregenerate people who have not come to Christ acknowledging him as their personal saviour. Whereas, those who are in the Spirit and living in a prominently spiritual way are, of course, the spiritual people. They are not only in the Spirit but are also living in accordance with the Spirit. They allow the Spirit to control their lives.

Finally, we have those who are in the Spirit but are living mostly in a natural way. These are Christians who, sadly, are living in lots of ways the same as unbelievers. They're in the Spirit (as to their salvation) but they are living in accord with the flesh or sin nature within them. This is where some attach the unfortunate label of 'carnal Christians' – although that should be a contradiction in terms. Never settle for that, although we may meet some who claim to be happily resigned to living with a foot in both camps. That's not at all God's plan. To see that, let's return to the first part of our reading from Romans chapter 8 and verses 3 and 4: *"For what the Law could not do, weak as it was through the flesh, God did: sending His own Son in the likeness of sinful flesh and as an offering for sin, He condemned sin in the flesh, so that the requirement of the Law might be fulfilled in us who do not walk according to the flesh but according to the Spirit."*

What was it that the Law could not do? Ah, you say, that's

easy! The Law could not of itself bring us salvation. Fine. But thinking back to our previous study, what exactly do you mean by salvation? Do you have our justification in mind or is it our sanctification? I would put it to you that what the Law could not do was it could not bring about our salvation in terms of our sanctification. Remember, this includes our response to our salvation. Why do I say this? Well, let's come to the ending of our reading: "*For what the Law could not do ... God did: sending His own Son ... so that the requirement of the Law might be fulfilled in us who do not walk according to the flesh but according to the Spirit.*" When the righteous requirement of the Law is fulfilled in the life of a Christian believer on the Lord Jesus, this means that person is living in accord with the Spirit. He or she is a spiritual person, someone who belongs to God's spiritual family and is overall living in a spiritual way. Let's all make that our ambition!

3

Is It a Case of 'No Holiness No Heaven'?

We may sometimes hear a catch-phrase such as 'no holiness, no heaven.' It may be supported by a verse such as Hebrews 12:14 that says that without holiness none shall see the Lord. But if we're to avoid the danger of proof-texting we need to know we are using that text in its appropriate context. The full context leading up to that verse in Hebrews is this:

> *"It is for discipline that you endure; God deals with you as with sons; for what son is there whom his father does not discipline? But if you are without discipline, of which all have become partakers, then you are illegitimate children and not sons. Furthermore, we had earthly fathers to discipline us, and we respected them; shall we not much more be subject to the Father of spirits, and live? For they disciplined us for a short time as seemed best to them, but He disciplines us for our good, so that we may share His holiness.*

> *For the moment, all discipline seems not to be pleasant,*

but painful; yet to those who have been trained by it, afterward it yields the peaceful fruit of righteousness. Therefore, strengthen the hands that are weak and the knees that are feeble, and make straight paths for your feet, so that the limb which is impaired may not be dislocated, but rather be healed. Pursue peace with all people, and the holiness without which no one will see the Lord" (Hebrews 12:7-14).

The writer here was addressing those who were genuine believers on the Lord Jesus. As such, they were finding the Christian life difficult, being full of hardships. It's very probable their own families had rejected these Jewish background believers of the first century. So, they were really struggling. Reassuringly, the writer urged them to view these challenges positively as part of God's training program for them. The imagery used is that of parents training up their children, even disciplining them in order for them to manage the trials of life that come later on.

The writer viewed such happenings not as being a strange thing but, on the contrary, as a validation of their genuine Christian testimony and their genuine relationship to the Lord. The trials we go through as followers of Christ are allowed by God with the intention that they should shape us to be more like Christ who suffered more than anyone in his life on earth. Trained by God's disciplining program, these believers by responding to it would come to 'see the Lord' through sharing more deeply in his holiness. Surely the setting here is about true followers of Christ becoming matured as disciples such that they walk with the Lord and enjoy fellowship with him, the very fellowship of his sufferings, in fact (see Philippians 3:10).

To attempt to sum this up as 'no holiness, no heaven' is quite misleading, I suggest. It's saying that setbacks and challenges are not a contrary sign for someone en route to heaven, because God can make use of any difficulty within his training program that promotes our becoming more holy in this life, more like his son, Jesus, and so more intimate with him. Without daily holiness there'll be no intimacy with Christ now for those who are definitely bound for heaven.

In the language we were using in a previous study, this section in Hebrews 12 is about our **response** to salvation, not about our **receiving** salvation. It's about **sanctification**, not about **justification**. This is about breaking the power of sin that's *already* cancelled. I think those who take the 'no holiness, no heaven' stance do so not because they believe our own good works play any role in making us acceptable to God, but rather they hold the 'no holiness, no heaven' view in an understandable desire to expose the problem of those who are making a spurious claim to heaven due to having made a false profession of Christ as their saviour in the first place.

On occasions, when I've preached the Gospel clearly to an audience where people already professed Christ, say at a Christian Bible camp, quite a few have come forward for counselling afterwards. Some had lacked full assurance; others had troubled consciences over continuing sinful practices; but there were some who, when hearing the Gospel in greater depth and clarity, concluded their previous profession wasn't true, wasn't real, and that was, in their case, the reason for there being no fruit in their lives. Our Lord in his teaching gave us the basic rule of knowing a person by their fruits, that is by the results seen in their life; in other words by the quality produced in their lifestyle. He said:

> *"Beware of the false prophets, who come to you in sheep's clothing, but inwardly are ravenous wolves. You will know them by their fruits. Grapes are not gathered from thorn bushes, nor figs from thistles, are they? So every good tree bears good fruit, but the bad tree bears bad fruit. A good tree cannot bear bad fruit, nor can a bad tree bear good fruit. Every tree that does not bear good fruit is cut down and thrown into the fire. So then, you will know them by their fruits. "Not everyone who says to Me, 'Lord, Lord,' will enter the kingdom of heaven, but the one who does the will of My Father who is in heaven will enter. Many will say to Me on that day, 'Lord, Lord, did we not prophesy in Your name, and in Your name cast out demons, and in Your name perform many miracles?' And then I will declare to them, 'I never knew you; LEAVE ME, YOU WHO PRACTICE LAWLESSNESS'"* (Matthew 7:15-23).

Those last words are most relevant to the headline question we're asking in these studies. And that question again is: can a person profess Christ and still be lost? Jesus himself declares there will be many who in the future will say to him, *"Lord, we prophesied and performed miracles in your name."* In saying this they were claiming a kind of allegiance to him. But his reply, as he anticipates here, will be, *"I never knew you."* We really must emphasise the word 'never' in that sentence where Jesus says *"I never knew you."*

I say that because it's never the case that someone whom the Lord knows in a saving sense can ever ultimately be rejected. He's promised never to cast out any who come to him (John 6:37). There's no contradiction with that here due to the presence of the word 'never' as in Jesus saying "I never knew them." These persons, sadly, will be lost because they never at any time had been found. That is, they never belonged to Christ, never had been drawn to him by the Father. Oh yes, they'd professed the Lord Jesus, but it's shown here to have been a false profession.

To sum up what we've been saying in this study: two lives may look similar to us, characterised by sinful habits and some questionable behaviours. There are two possibilities. Either, we're dealing with a genuine believer who has quenched the Holy Spirit within them (1 Thessalonians 5:19); or, this is someone who is merely a nominal Christian, their profession being shallow and spurious. For them Christianity is about ticking boxes, following rules and hoping that their best is good enough. The trouble is they've never seen the depravity of their heart. They've had no true experience of the grace of God leading them to repentance. They've never been made alive in a work that can only be done by God.

I think it was evangelist Billy Graham who once said that walking into a garage doesn't make you into a motor car, and walking into a church building – even attending regularly – doesn't make you to be a born-again Christian. Then there's what I refer to as 'the biggest lie in the world.' I call it that because wherever in the world I visit I encounter this lie in one form or another. What is it? It's this: people say that when you get to heaven's door, God's going to weigh up all the good you've ever done in your life, then weigh up all the bad you've done, and if the good outweighs the bad, he'll let you into his heaven.

Let me say this plainly: that's not, never, nowhere the teaching of the Bible. That's not the Good News Jesus preached nor later his Apostles after him. That's not the record they left behind for us in the New Testament of our Bibles. One place in the Bible where people could conceivably – but wrongly – draw that conclusion is from part of John's Gospel where it says this: "*Do not be amazed at this; for a time is coming when all who are in the tombs will hear His voice, and will come out: those who did the good deeds to a resurrection of life, those who committed the bad deeds to a resurrection of judgment*" (John 5:28-29).

By way of analogy, I want you to think of what we sometimes hear about medical studies. For example, one may be summed up as saying that there's a correlation between eating certain foods and contracting certain illnesses. Notice, we said 'correlation.' That doesn't yet mean that a causal link – a cause and effect relationship – has been established. The one doesn't necessarily lead to the other. And no more so here. For sure, there's a correlation between those who are found doing good works and those who are raised to life in the future. But their good works are not the cause of their good resurrection. Not at all. Rather it's the faith that lies at the root of their good works. A nearby verse makes it so clear. Jesus says in John 5:24: "*... I say to you, the one who hears My word, and believes Him who sent Me, has eternal life, and does not come into judgment, but has passed out of death into life*" (John 5:24).

There it is: after repenting of our sins, what must we do to be saved from judgement by God for our sins? The answer from the Bible is: *"Believe on the Lord Jesus"* (Acts 17:31).

4

Are Good Works Required for Salvation?

Not all commentators – including some very notable ones – have been kind to James, the apostle who wrote a Bible letter found towards the back of our Bibles. His lack of focus on the person of Christ or on the person of the Holy Spirit are among the reasons usually quoted, but then there's the added charge that his theology may be suspect as it seems to run counter to Paul's - especially in the matter of faith and works. But alleged contradictions in the Bible need to be carefully checked. One author[1] has taken every supposed contradiction posted on the Internet and convincingly shown not one of them stands up to close logical scrutiny. We'll see that the same certainly applies to this one about the supposed conflict between the apostles James and Paul.

We'll begin then by posing the question: is James preaching salvation by God's grace alone or is he preaching salvation by works? Before we begin to answer that, we should straightaway

---

[1]   Jason Lisle, Keeping Faith in an Age of Reason, Master Books, 2017

affirm that the inclusion of James in the canon of Scripture – in other words the fact that it's included in our Bibles – means that we must start from the premise that this is part of God's inspired Word, and as a result is inerrant (i.e. without error) in what it teaches. Once we grant that, we'll easily see that James can be understood as in no way contradicting Paul. The section that's caused confusion for at least some people is found in James chapter 2, starting from verse 14. James says: *"What use is it, my brethren, if someone says he has faith but he has no works? Can that faith save him?"*

Then, having asked the question, James proceeds to give 4 answers – the first of which highlights a practical absurdity. Let James take it up from here: *"If a brother or sister is without clothing and in need of daily food, and one of you says to them, "Go in peace, be warmed and be filled," and yet you do not give them what is necessary for their body, what use is that? Even so faith, if it has no works, is dead, being by itself"* (James 2:15-17).

Obviously, the intended answer to the question 'What's the use of withholding practical help?' is 'No use at all.' Remember the bigger question under consideration is: 'Can faith without works save anyone?' The faith, if we can call it that, that simply dismisses a destitute brother or sister without practical assistance – meaning faith without works – is not real faith at all. God is a God of means. Practical help is no faith-killer, but the absence of such support is a denial of true or real faith.

Now, James brings us answer number two by considering two competing challenges: "But someone may *well* say, 'You have faith and I have works; show me your faith without the works, and I will show you my faith by my works.'" (James 2:18). The first thing here is about being asked how we could show faith without producing works as the supporting evidence of that faith; and the second thing is about showing works as the real evidence of the faith behind them. These head-to-head challenges distinguish between what's real and what's only hot air or empty words. We can conclude that the faith that saves is real faith that's able to be displayed through faith-motivated actions. If we've nothing to show for the faith we claim to have then neither is there any faith there. No works, no faith.

Next, or thirdly, James employs an extreme example, when he says: *"You believe that God is one. You do well; the demons also believe, and shudder. But are you willing to recognize ... that faith without works is useless?"* (James 2:19-20). I called it an extreme example, and it is! Do demons believe? Yes, in the sense that they intellectually know that God exists. But does that faith save them? No, it doesn't, and neither would you expect it to. A mere awareness of the facts, a mental assent to the truth, is not what faith is all about. Faith, real faith, truly exists when you act on the facts.

The fourth and final response James gives to the question of whether faith without works is saving faith is to quote some historical examples of faith from two famous lives in the Bible. Here's what he says:

> *"Was not Abraham our father justified by works when he offered up Isaac his son on the altar? You see that faith was working with his works, and as a result of the works, faith was perfected; and the Scripture was fulfilled*

which says, "AND ABRAHAM BELIEVED GOD, AND IT WAS RECKONED TO HIM AS RIGHTEOUSNESS," and he was called the friend of God. You see that a man is justified by works and not by faith alone. In the same way, was not Rahab the harlot also justified by works when she received the messengers and sent them out by another way? For just as the body without the spirit is dead, so also faith without works is dead" (James 2:21-26).

Let's take that example of Abraham, because it's the one where people have sensed that James is saying something different from Paul. James quotes Genesis 15:6 (as does Paul, which says): "*AND ABRAHAM BELIEVED GOD, AND IT WAS RECKONED TO HIM AS RIGHTEOUSNESS.*" This is from part of Abraham's story, long before the most famous event in Abraham's life – when he was prepared to offer up his son, Isaac, as a sacrifice. We know chapter 15 is a long time before this because Isaac wasn't even born back then when we're told Abraham's faith was the basis for him being reckoned as righteous by God. But when God tested the genuineness of his faith years later by asking him to sacrifice his precious, long-awaited son, Abraham so trusted God that he wouldn't hold back anything precious. Of course, God would never have let him go through with the act of killing his son; it was simply a test in which God knew Abraham's faith would triumph.

In that sense he was justified by his works – only in the sense that his work of being prepared to offer his son proved the real faith that he previously had. As James said: "*You see that faith was working with his works, and as a result of the works, faith was perfected.*" We need to understand that James is not contrasting faith with works as to which may save us. We know from Paul's biblical writings that the answer is clear: we are saved or justified by faith. James' point is totally consistent with that. What he tells us is that a mere professed faith can't save us, only a real faith. And what's more: any real faith will inevitably be vindicated by works – being the actions which stem from our faith.

Someone has put it this way: James here is using the word 'justify' in a different sense from the way Paul uses it. James uses it in the more or less everyday sense in which we might use it; whereas Paul uses it in a technical and biblical sense of being declared not guilty; more than that, of being declared righteous. James as we say, by contrast, uses it here in the sense of us when we talk of justifying our beliefs or opinions. For example, if things turn out as we suspected they might, we would feel justified in the sense of our view being vindicated by how events turned out. It's only through our faith in Christ that the Bible tells us we are justified in God's sight and so ready for heaven. Only faith, but it must be real faith – not an empty profession.

In the 19th century there was a tightrope stunt artist known professionally as the "The Great Blondin." In 1859, he was the first person to walk across on a 335-metre rope suspended high over the water of the Niagara Falls in Canada, which plunged down far below him. On one occasion, he asked the crowd, "How many of you believe that I, The Great Blondin, can not only walk back across that tightrope, but this time do it while I push a wheelbarrow?" They cried, "We believe! We believe!" Then he asked, "How many of you really believe it?" "Oh, we really believe it!" they shouted back. One man, a little more enthusiastic than the others, caught The Great Blondin's eye. Pointing to the man, he said, "If you really believe, then get in the wheelbarrow." The man quickly disappeared. The difference between what we say we believe and what we really do believe shows up in our actions.

It's striking that Paul bookends his letter to the Romans with an identical phrase, *"the obedience of faith"* (Romans 1:5 and Romans 16:26). He begins by saying he'd received apostleship to bring about *the* obedience of faith among all the Gentiles. This was the goal of Paul's preaching. The ending of Paul's letter to the Romans contains the same expression: *"the preaching of Jesus Christ ... leading to obedience of faith."* Such a thing as 'easy believe-ism' – in other words, just believe – wasn't known to Paul. The Gospel, once accepted, should shape our whole life.

An authority on New Testament Greek, Robertson, says of both these occurrences that this is the obedience which springs from faith. Faith, self-renouncing trust in Jesus Christ, is obedience to the gospel command to believe on the Lord Jesus Christ for salvation ... and that faith in Jesus Christ initiates a believer into a life of obedience to Jesus Christ. Faith is not mere notional assent to biblical propositions. **Real faith always has works of obedience. It's faith alone that saves, but the faith that saves is not alone.**

5

Is It Possible to Fall Away?

Hebrews chapter 6 tells us about it being impossible for God to lie. There is, however, another 'impossible thing' found in this chapter. Let's read about it from verse 4:

> *"For in the case of those who have once been enlightened and have tasted of the heavenly gift and have been made partakers of the Holy Spirit and have tasted the good word of God and the powers of the age to come, and then have fallen away, it is impossible to renew them again to repentance, since they again crucify to themselves the Son of God and put Him to open shame. For ground that drinks the rain which often falls on it and brings forth vegetation useful to those for whose sake it is also tilled, receives a blessing from God; but if it yields thorns and thistles, it is worthless and close to being cursed, and it ends up being burned"* (Hebrews 6:4-8).

What's this second impossibility? The fact that it's impossible to renew to repentance those who are described as 'falling away'

28

after they've become partakers of the Holy Spirit. This is a difficult verse. Some explain it by making out that the people in question were never truly saved, but that they were only false professors of a salvation that was never really theirs. But isn't it made clear that they'd received the Holy Spirit, and they'd been enlightened? Theirs had been a real experience of God's gift, God's Word and God's power. So where does that leave us? Are we forced after all to conclude that these genuine believers could indeed fall away from their salvation? No. The words of the Lord Jesus in John's Gospel chapter 10 ought to be a sufficient defence against such thinking. There we read that he gives his sheep eternal life, and they'll never perish (v.28). God's gifts are irrevocable, Paul adds in Romans chapter 11 (verse 29). He'll never call back or take back the gift of salvation from anyone who's received it.

The only possible answer as to what this passage in Hebrews 6 means – and there's another one like it in Hebrews 10 – is that there's something else from which these Hebrew Christians were capable of falling away. From the surrounding content of the letter, this is certainly the case. For these early Jewish Christians were wavering under pressure. They were tempted to leave the New Testament churches of God with which they were now associated and go back to the old ways of Judaism. Some were considering leaving this Fellowship of companions of Jesus the Messiah (Hebrews 1:9).

The writer has already warned them not to repeat the mistake of their ancestors who'd come up out of slavery in Egypt but had failed to arrive in the promised land of rest. A whole generation had perished in the desert, because they'd turned back to Egypt in their hearts. The warning was clear: if these Hebrew Christians were to actually leave the Community of New Testament believers in the first century churches of God, and turn back to serving under the Law of Moses, there would be no way they could come back again into the Community of the local churches of God then. For they would have repeated the sin of the Jewish nation in rejecting Christ as the Messiah.

In support of this understanding, let's unpack the textual illustration from nature that follows in the words we've already read. It's one that provides further explanation of the true meaning of falling away. Sometimes, when rain falls on the earth, instead of yielding useful, nourishing plants, reflecting God's blessing, it brings forth thorns and briars, "near to being cursed, whose end is to be burned." The words *"whose end is to be burned"* must have brought the first readers of this letter up sharply. We're dealing here with the horrifying possibility of believers openly and aggressively repudiating their faith and profession, so that they exclude themselves from the possibility of repentance. The only prospect for them is inevitable divine judgement. But is this the judgement of eternal fire, as some might be inclined to assume because of the analogy of the burning of the worthless thorns and briars? No! It is the burning of what the land produces, not of the land itself.

This biblical illustration helps us understand that it's what's produced in a Christian's life that may be burned, his works, and not the believer himself. Our security is not involved here. That's safe in the Lord's keeping. Do we then have guidance elsewhere in the New Testament that takes into account the fearful thought of destruction by burning? Well, yes, we have.

ln 1 Corinthians chapter 3 we have a description of building for God in a believer's life, building on the foundation of Jesus Christ a life of service, the value of which may vary widely. There's mention of gold, silver, precious stones, wood, hay, stubble. The descent in order of value becomes ever more steep until we arrive at stubble in all its worthlessness. The analogy is with the life of a person whose service is described in this way, *"If anyone's work is burned he will suffer loss; but he himself will be saved, yet so as through fire"* (v.15).

This remains a timely warning. While serving as a community of Christians, there are – as this chapter calls them – "things that accompany salvation" (Hebrews 6:9). Things connected with an understanding of the priesthood of the Lord Jesus, and his current service in heaven on behalf of believers on earth whose gatherings are in accord with what the Bible teaches. We would, then, acknowledge that the Bible talks of a 'falling away' being possible, but the big question is: a falling away from what? To understand this in context, we have to distinguish between our **salvation** and our accompanying **service** for the Lord. The Bible, when we understand it correctly, is saying that it's possible to fall away only from a position of responsibility in serving God. It's not at all saying that we can fall away from our eternally secure status as being forever saved from the penalty of our sins. The theme of the Hebrews' letter is our **service**, and not our **salvation.**

In its first century Jewish setting, the Hebrews' letter referred to the danger of early Jewish believers being drawn back into following the old ways of Judaism again. In that first century setting, there could be no recovery back into church of God fellowship for anyone who renounced Jesus as Messiah and returned to the old ways of Judaism (such was the high profile damage to the testimony that it was in effect a re-crucifying of Christ, see Hebrews 10:29-31). Such would be a disastrous U-turn, after they'd had the courage to publicly recognize Jesus as the true Messiah.

The theme of Hebrews is not whether these wavering Jews maintained their salvation, but whether they maintained their place of privilege among God's worshiping people – or fell away from it. How can we be sure that this is what Hebrews is saying? Well, the letter itself – actually in chapter 3, verse 6 – describes them as being God's house (along with all the other New Testament believers in the churches of God in all the different localities we read about). The first place to start, then, would seem to be by asking 'What exactly is God's House?' The writer tells the original recipients of this letter that they're God's house. Linking himself with them, he says *"whose house we are"* - and then he adds the condition: *"if we hold fast ..."*

Now that's the point I want you to especially notice with me. There's a condition here. Therefore, God's house – which Hebrews teaches is conditional – cannot be identified with the vast company of all those who've ever known salvation by God's grace through personal faith in Jesus Christ, and is in fact also to be distinguished even from all currently living believers – because of that stated condition. The defining issue for a place in God's house is not the possession of salvation, for although Hebrews tells us we can fall away from God's house, yet we've checked the Bible tells us we can never be dispossessed of our salvation. There's no need whatsoever for us to hold fast to our salvation, for the Lord Jesus himself holds us fast, and assures us none can snatch us away from him. But, regarding what's called God's house, we evidently *do* need to hold fast, just as they did, to whom the author of Hebrews wrote some 2000 years ago.

The Hebrews' letter was written to early Jewish Christians who'd left behind the ceremonial Law of Moses to embrace Jesus as the Messiah and follow the teaching of his apostles. By following the apostles' teaching they found themselves in the New Testament Churches of God. The Book of the Acts of the Apostles documents exactly how this came about. The existence of these churches spread outwards from Jerusalem particularly as a result of the various missionary journeys of the Apostle Paul.

Those who turned to the Lord in each place were subsequently numbered and identified with the church of God in that locality. Now, what's very significant is these local churches weren't just left to go their own way. They were linked by visits from the likes of Paul; they were addressed together in several of the Bible letters; they sent relief aid to one another as needs arose; and they were bound by a common adherence to the same understanding of the Lord's teaching – a point clearly demonstrated in the case of the Jerusalem Council of Acts chapter 15 (but see also 1 Corinthians 4:17; 7:17). In other words, they were an inter-linked community of disciples, maintained by the church elders in the different localities working in close fellowship with each other (1 Peter 1:1;5:1).

There isn't the slightest evidence that some practised baptism while others didn't; no indication whatsoever that some churches had elders whereas others had a different form of government (Acts 14:22). They were united in belief and practice as a model community, and this is what's described as being 'God's house' on earth. But just as in some parts of the world today, they were a persecuted community then. And some of them, by the time that the letter to the Hebrews came to be written, had come to feel life would be easier outside of this Messianic community, life would be simpler again if, as in the old days, they were just going along with the Law of Moses like the majority of folks around them, at least in Israel. To people just like that, the writer of the Hebrews' letter makes his appeal by the Spirit of God: 'don't go back; don't fall away.' To quit their association with the practising Christian community would not mean the loss of their salvation, but – and this is the main point of the letter – they'd miss out on everything that was special in serving God together in the biblical community of Churches of God.

6

It's Not About How To Be Saved

The Apostle John, when writing the Gospel that bears his name, leaves us in no doubt as to his purpose in writing it. He tells us it was so that its readers might believe Jesus is the Son of God and, by believing that, have eternal life in his name (John 20:31). The same author is equally candid about his motivation for writing his first letter, the one we know as 1 John, towards the back of our Bibles. He wrote it so that those who already believe may know, and be assured, that they have eternal life (1 John 5:13).

John's repeated message in that first letter is that those who 'believe' may 'know.' In chapter 2 verse 3, he speaks of 'knowing Him [Jesus]' and then goes on to speak of *"knowing that we are in Him"* (v.5); and later of *"knowing we are of God and of the truth"* (5:19; 4:6; 3:19). Finally in his last chapter, he speaks about *"knowing that we have eternal life"* (5:13). You see what I mean about his theme being 'knowing with certainty'?

John, it seems, liked dealing with certainties. Actually, it appears he wrote about what we might call a double certainty in his first

35

letter: namely, both the **objective** and the **subjective** certainty of Gospel truth. What do I mean by that? Take first the matter of the objective truth of the Gospel. John gives us 3 supports for this: he cites the testimony of history by referring to the birth, life and death of Jesus; also, the apostolic testimony as those apostles of whom he was one, who had prolonged contact with Christ at close quarters; and finally, the testimony of the Spirit with whom believers to the present day have been anointed as internal witness to the truth of the Gospel.

Then there's the other matter of the subjective certainty of the Gospel. How can I be sure that those Gospel blessings are mine, that I've taken full possession of them? That I belong to God as one of his children, with all my sins forgiven, and that I'm the sure possessor of eternal life? Basically, John says, and says repeatedly throughout his letter, that there are again 3 ways of knowing this: that is, of being sure that we have eternal life. These are the tests of continuing to hold our beliefs; keeping the Lord's commands; and loving one another. Here are examples of how John uses these tests: *"The one who believes in the Son of God has the testimony in himself; the one who does not believe God has made Him a liar, because he has not believed in the testimony that God has given concerning His Son"* (1 John 5:10).

That's about maintaining our convictions. But we also read: *"By this we know that we have come to know Him, if we keep His commandments"* (1 John 2:3). That's about doing what's right, and therefore doing all that the Lord says. And then we read: *"Beloved, let's love one another; for love is from God, and everyone who loves has been born of God and knows God"* (1 John 4:7). That's clearly about loving one another – the third test that when we comply with it, as with the other two, enables us to enjoy certainty as to who we are and where we're going: a saved sinner bound for eternal glory with Christ.

So, recapping then, in John's first letter we find he gives three assurances for the certainty of knowing, through faith, that we've been born into God's spiritual family and, as a result, possess eternal life. This is such a relevant message because many people today speak of hoping they'll be acceptable to God and one day enter into life in God's presence. John, however, writes of knowledge that is certain. He gives, as we've said, three ways by which we can be sure that we are already eternally secure: and these are by believing; by obeying; and by loving.

The first way is about maintaining our deep conviction in the truth about Jesus, the Son of God. Again and again in chapter five alone, he stresses that it's those who *"believe in the Son of God"* (vv.5,10,13) who know they have eternal life. Sadly, some believers, by losing faith, lose the assurance of their salvation - even though they can't lose salvation itself. The second assurance is by means of keeping the Lord's commands and doing the things that are right (3:9,10). Among the things John writes aimed at helping us really know that we have eternal life (5:13) is this matter of keeping the Lord commandments. Earlier, as though to reinforce that, he's already said: *"Whoever has been born of God does not sin, for His seed remains in him; and he cannot sin, because he has been born of God. In this the children of God and the children of the devil are manifest: Whoever does not practice righteousness is not of God"* (1 John 3:9-10 NKJV).

Now, it's not that this means we should be sinless, for John has already told us that "if we say that we have no sin, we deceive ourselves." The sense is most likely that those who are born-again would rather choose not to sin rather than it being the case that they cannot sin (compare Mark 6:5). Consistent with our new nature, the practice of righteousness ought to characterize those who are God's children, and be typical of them. When that's the case, it all serves as further assurance to our own hearts of a work of God's grace that's been done there.

The third way of assurance of someone having been born into God's family and possessing eternal life is the business of loving one another (4:7,8). Remember, John has said at the beginning of chapter five, we've mentioned it already, but we'll quote it again: "*... everyone who loves Him who begot also loves him who is begotten of Him. By this we know that we love the children of God, when we love God and keep His commandments*" (1 John 5:1-2 NKJV).

To see how strongly this matter of loving one another comes over as an assurance of our new birth and possession of eternal life, we only have to read some more verses from the previous chapter:

> "*Beloved, let us love one another, for love is of God; and everyone who loves is born of God and knows God. He who does not love does not know God, for God is love*" (1 John 4:7-8 NKJV).

> "*If someone says, 'I love God,' and hates his brother, he is a liar; for he who does not love his brother whom he has seen, how can he love God whom he has not seen? And*

*this commandment we have from Him: that he who loves
God must love his brother also"* (1 John 4:20–21 NKJV).

So there we have it: the certainty that the believer has eternal life. It's a certainty that's triply assured when we retain our convictions about the person of the Lord Jesus, and keep his commandments, and love each other. These things John has written to those of us who believe in the name of the Son of God, so that we may know we have eternal life. How wonderful to have a strong, a threefold assurance of the certainty of having a place in God's family and of being the possessor of eternal life.

Just so there's no misunderstanding, let me say again that John's theme here is not salvation itself, but the **assurance** of salvation. It's not about how to be saved, but it is about how to be sure we're saved. Keeping the commandments and loving each other are not things we've got to do so as to be saved, or remain saved, from the judgement of our sins; but if we are saved by faith, and we do these things, they'll help us to maintain the certainty of our convictions.

7

Is It Possible to Believe the Gospel in Vain?

The Apostle Paul wrote to the local church of God at Corinth and said: "*Now I would remind you, brothers, of the gospel I preached to you, which you received, in which you stand, and by which you are being saved, if you hold fast to the word I preached to you—unless you believed in vain*" (1 Corinthians 15:1-2 ESV). What are these verses telling us? At first sight they seem to say that those who receive the gospel are only saved if they hold fast to what they've believed, and there's a possibility that if people waver in their belief they may lose their salvation. That conclusion would be deeply unsettling to many Christians, who might feel insecure in their faith and uncertain about their status before God.

Before jumping to such an apparently reasonable conclusion we should consider the basic rule for understanding the Bible: that Scripture itself should be the interpreter of Scripture. In other words, having established the overall teaching of the Bible on a particular point, we should attempt to interpret any 'difficult' texts in the light of that. It's always safe to allow verses that can be plainly understood to guide us in our approach to understanding other verses where the meaning at first reading seems more obscure.

In this example at the beginning of 1 Corinthians 15, there's a wealth of Bible verses that assure us that the transformation brought about in us when we exercise personal faith in Christ is both instantaneous and irreversible. For example, Jesus said: *"Whoever hears my word and believes him who sent me has eternal life. He does not come into judgment, but has passed from death to life"* (John 5:24). What this verse says can additionally be understood to be irreversible, because elsewhere in the Bible (e.g. 1 Corinthians 12:13) we learn that the believer is incorporated into Christ, becoming a member of the universal church where all who've ever believed in Christ are described metaphorically as being Christ's body. Doesn't that settle it? For how can we imagine Christ being dismembered? In addition to that, chapter two of Ephesians gives us the whole argument:

> *"... you were dead in the trespasses and sins in which you once walked, following the course of this world, following the prince of the power of the air, the spirit that is now at work in the sons of disobedience — But God, being rich in mercy, because of the great love with which he loved us ... even when we were dead in our trespasses, made us alive together with Christ—by grace you have been saved—and raised us up with him and seated us with him in the heavenly places in Christ Jesus, so that in the coming ages he might show the immeasurable riches of his grace in kindness toward us in Christ Jesus. For by grace you have been saved through faith. And this is not*

your own doing; it is the gift of God, not a result of works, so that no one may boast. For we are his workmanship, created in Christ Jesus for good works, which God prepared beforehand, that we should walk in them."

It is very clear, therefore, that our salvation from the penalty of sin is a work of God, underwritten by his power and love. What, then, does the earlier quoted passage from the opening of First Corinthians chapter 15 mean? Let's remind ourselves of it again. The Apostle Paul wrote to the local church of God at Corinth and said: *"Now I would remind you, brothers, of the gospel I preached to you, which you received, in which you stand, and by which you are being saved, if you hold fast to the word I preached to you—unless you believed in vain"* (1 Corinthians 15:1-2 ESV).

The quote comes from the English Standard version, which uses the expression *"by which you are being saved"* – in other words, it uses a continuous sense of the verb. This is a better translation of the original than some other Bible translations because the action being described here does strictly relate to a continuing action. Most newer Bible translations recognise this. But we've seen that eternal salvation is the instantaneous and irrevocable work of God — so how can we understand this continuous sense of being saved? Well, the first possible answer is something we've come across in an earlier study: and that is that the word 'salvation' is used in different parts of the Bible in two different senses, firstly referring to being declared not guilty, even righteous before God (justification); and secondly to our being rescued from sin in our present life (sanctification).

This first solution, then, that we might offer in trying to

correctly understand 1 Corinthians 15 is to suggest that these people were saved in the sense of being justified, but were not being saved in the sense of leading a sanctified life – and so were back-sliders. Their profession was a true one, but they were no longer living up to it. Their belief was in vain only in the sense of producing a life that had lately become empty of such good results as ought to accompany salvation.

Much of the rest of chapter 15 relates to the resurrection of Christ, and also of believers. This is an essential part of Christian faith, but some in Corinth would seem to have begun to doubt it, so Paul had to remind them to hold fast what they'd believed. We ask again, 'How could they believe *in vain?*' Another angle from which to come at this is to note that believing in vain means believing 'frivolously' or 'casually.' Anyone who believed in this way may not have really understood the full significance of their profession; meaning that it wasn't a real saving faith at all. Paul's words would make his hearers examine themselves, to test the genuineness of their faith. In other words, this second solution is to offer the explanation that these people never had a real saving faith that had ever justified them in the first place.

So far where we've got to is: either these people being addressed by Paul were true believers who'd ceased to do the things that pleased the Lord, or perhaps they'd never ever made a true profession of faith. It was only an outward show, a going along with the crowd. Anyone in that category might well be expected to question the fundamental reality of the Christian teaching of resurrection.

But may I offer a third possible solution? It's one, I must say, that I'm more inclined to accept. As we said, we must compare scripture with scripture or one verse with another. Let's explore if reading these early verses of 1 Corinthians 15 in the context of the verses that follow shortly after them is a special case of this. I suggest to you that it's instructive to read verses 12-14 as an expansion on verse 2. Again using the ESV, here are verses 1 and 2: *"Now I would remind you, brothers, of the gospel I preached to you, which you received, in which you stand, and by which you are being saved, if you hold fast to the word I preached to you—unless you believed in vain."* Could it be that what is there stated with great economy is later expanded upon? Let's look down the chapter to verse 11:

> *"Whether then it was I or they, so we preach and so you believed. Now if Christ is proclaimed as raised from the dead, how can some of you say that there is no resurrection of the dead? But if there is no resurrection of the dead, then not even Christ has been raised. And if Christ has not been raised, then our preaching is in vain and your faith is in vain. We are even found to be misrepresenting God, because we testified about God that he raised Christ, whom he did not raise if it is true that the dead are not raised. For if the dead are not raised, not even Christ has been raised. And if Christ has not been raised, your faith is futile and you are still in your sins"* (1 Corinthians 15:11-17).

Here once again we end up with the verdict that their faith was futile. But we now have more information. I suggest, therefore, that for many among them Paul or others had preached *"Jesus and the resurrection"* (see Acts 17:18) and so they'd arrived at an effective faith in the true Gospel and as a result of that also had an enduring salvation. However, others had later come among them at Corinth, people whose system of belief maintained there was no human resurrection. Paul effectively points out that preaching like this is effectively preaching and believing in a false Gospel – one in which Christ himself was not raised. In which case, belief in such a different, false Gospel was indeed, and is still, a futile thing; for a dead Christ cannot save a sinner from his or her sins.

We've presented three ways of reading this difficult text. None of them contradicts other plain Bible verses that teach us authoritatively that no-one who truly professes Christ as saviour can ever lose that salvation, even if they later backslide. But equally it's true, and witnessed to in other places in the Bible, that someone who has falsely professed Christ will not be saved. They remain eternally lost. It's not that they lose salvation, for they were never at any time truly saved. Lastly, there's the option (also shown to be realistic in Galatians 1:6-8) that a person can sincerely believe in something that's not true, not the genuine Gospel, but a travesty of the truth. Faith in the wrong thing saves no-one.

8

Once Saved, Always Saved

In the same way that we might make use of recognized land-marks in giving someone directions, it's just as necessary to identify the Bible's main or landmark teachings and then navigate our way around individual and sometimes difficult verses in relation to them. If our understanding of a particular text seems to be at odds with one of the Bible's main teachings, it may indicate that the text should be related to a different teaching instead.

One such landmark teaching is that a truly born-again person through faith in Jesus is secure in God's keeping so far as his salvation from eternal judgement is concerned. Such a person is seen as 'in Christ' (a phrase found about 80 times in the King James Version of the New Testament), a status granted when he or she first believed and was *"blessed with every spiritual blessing in the heavenly places in Christ Jesus"* (Ephesians 1:3,4). As Christ himself confirmed: *"the one who comes to Me I will certainly not cast out ... this is the will of Him who sent Me, that of all that He has given Me I lose nothing"* (John 6:37-39).

But there's another equally clear landmark teaching which is that as the believer travels daily nearer his assured heavenly home he or she's accountable to the Lord Jesus for their response to the will of God. These two landmark biblical teachings are distinct but complementary. The first of these two lines of teaching gives the believer the utmost assurance of salvation from his deserved eternal judgement in the lake of fire; but the other establishes that such grace in salvation mustn't be lightly regarded. We need to add on our part all diligence, in our faith supplying virtue, knowledge, self-control, patience, godliness and love of the brethren (2 Peter 1:5-8).

With these two truths of Scripture as background, let's now consider some specific verses. 1 Timothy 1:19-20 talks about two persons being *"handed over to Satan."* This we may understand as the excommunication of these two men from the first century churches of God. Once they'd been debarred from local church fellowship, they'd experience the full effect of Satan's false teachings.

Then in 1 Corinthians 9:27, Paul says he disciplined his body so that he wouldn't be disqualified, which means to *"fail the test."* In this context, the test in question is the test of faithfulness in ministry (as in 2 Corinthians 13:5). There's no thought of the preacher himself being disqualified from heaven; that's not in the context here.

Then there's Matthew 24:13 with its mention of enduring to the end and being saved. But read the surrounding verses and see that they refer to the future period known to Bible students as the Great Tribulation. For future ones who come to know the

Lord – not us – this text will assure them that God will intervene to bring the tribulation to a timely end. Some of them will endure physically to the end of it, others will die, but as Luke 21:18 says *"not a hair of their head will perish."* Ultimate salvation is more than life and death in this age.

In John 15:6, Christ presents himself as the True Vine and describes believers in himself as being the branches. It's an illustration of communion with Christ and the fruitfulness it produces. The imagery serves to make the point that apart from him we can do nothing. There can be no fruitfulness if the individual believer's link of communion with Christ is broken. A disciple who fails to maintain this communion becomes like a withered vine branch, fit only to be burned. But not meaning the eternal burnings, the subject of eternal salvation is not under discussion here. The Lord, remember, was speaking to disciples about fruit-bearing: this is simply the case of no more fruit-bearing in the life of an unproductive backslider.

Then Peter, in 2 Peter 2:1-22, wrote of those who deny the Master that bought them (v.1) and so bring upon themselves swift destruction in this life, even a spiritual destruction. The last verses refer to disciples who have made progress to the extent of escaping the defilements of the world, but then have turned back. Even their present experience would now be worse for them than if they'd never known the way of righteousness – because troubled by a guilty conscience, and tormented with remorse for wasted opportunity, the backsliding believer often runs to greater excesses than someone who's not known the Lord.

And finally in this review of challenging Bible texts that can all be navigated with reference to the landmark of our accountability in service – and not with reference to our status in Christ – we perhaps ought to come to Matthew 12:31 with its mention of the unforgivable sin of blasphemy against the Holy Spirit. This has troubled so many believers who've wondered if they've committed the unforgivable sin and so lost their salvation. This verse, too, must be kept carefully in its special historical context. Jewish religious leaders were standing face to face with Christ. They'd witnessed his mighty miracles and good deeds, and yet very deliberately they'd attributed the power of the Holy Spirit by which Christ performed his cures to the power of Satan himself. That was the defiant sin of the Christ-rejecter. There's no comparable situation today which a believer could face.

So, overall, we need to relate difficult verses to established landmark teachings, and we must also interpret difficult verses in the light of plainer ones. The difficult texts are simplified once we observe key distinctions. Let's summarize: John 3:16 and Romans 6:23 make plain that God's free gift to the believer is eternal life. Romans 11:29 teaches a clear principle which is that God never asks for his gifts back (since he never makes mistakes in the first place). John 10:27-29 emphasizes that the believer (one of Christ's sheep) will never perish. That security depends on the strength of his love, not ours. The verses make plain the matter of our eternal security is in his hands (and the Father's hands), and not in our hands. Nothing can slip between his 'fingers,' we might say. He cannot lose his grip.

1 Corinthians 3:15 is interesting because it is about the judgement-seat of Christ where we (along with all believers

in Christ) will appear after we meet the Lord in the air. The purpose of appearing there will be so that our service here can be assessed (see 1 Corinthians 4:5; 2 Corinthians 5:10). We may fail to gain rewards and as much praise as we should, but we will still be saved *"though so as through fire."* The fire can burn up our works and reward, but not our gift of salvation itself.

There are many biblical ways of viewing our eternal security and they are all consistent. Our new birth is an irreversible process (as the choice of imagery would indicate). At salvation we become members of Christ's Church, called his Body. The power of Hades cannot prevail against it (Matthew 16:18) so as to dismember anyone. Also, the Bible has a lot to say about God's sovereignty, and this is the final absolute guarantee that our salvation can never be lost.

I'd like us to conclude with a reference to what's been called the 'Golden chain.' It's found in Romans chapter 8 where Paul talks about those *"whom He predestined, He also called; and these whom He called, He also justified; and these whom He justified, He also glorified"* (Romans 8:30). That's an unbreakable chain spanning from eternity to eternity, starting out from the wonderful reality we've been considering of our having been chosen in Christ.

This is God's plan for each Christian believer and it's one that gives confirmation of our eternal security in Christ. And there are four links in this unbreakable chain. The predestined are those who are called *"the called"* (1 Corinthians 1:24); and are again the same as those who are justified, and are also those who will be glorified. The same persons are in view at each stage. It's interesting to note that the final one, glorified, is set in the past tense although it clearly hasn't yet happened. That just goes to show that it's certain to happen, so much so that God treats it as already having taken place. That underlines the fact that no-one who begins it is going to fail to complete this four-stage journey. We're secure in Christ, from eternity to eternity. Not only is Christ to be glorified in us, but we're glorified in Christ (2 Thessalonians 1:12). That's even more remarkable, and is the ultimate display of our sanctification. We'll then be as much like Christ as it's possible for created beings to be.

"All things" are to be given to those (*"us all"*) for whom Christ was delivered up (v.32). This refers back to those already described as predestined, called, justified and glorified. Only those who start off as having been given by the Father to the Son will receive all things. Christ's death will be fully effective for all those for whom it was intended to be so.

9

The Different Tenses of Our Salvation

Salvation, as presented in the Bible, is threefold. By that I mean that there are three things we are saved from. The Bible teaches us about: salvation from sin's penalty, then salvation that's from sin's power, and finally, salvation from sin's presence. The first is once for all; the second is day by day; and we're still waiting for the third at the Lord's return. Let's explore then in order, starting with:

Salvation from Sin's Penalty (Eph.2:8,9)

This is where we take our first Bible reading:

> *"But God, being rich in mercy, because of His great love with which He loved us, even when we were dead in our transgressions, made us alive together with Christ (by grace you have been saved) ... and raised us up with Him, and seated us with Him in the heavenly places in Christ Jesus ... For by grace you have been saved through faith; and that not of yourselves, it is the gift of God; not as a*

result of works, so that no one may boast" (Ephesians 2:4-6, 8-9).

When that last verse talks about how we can be saved by God's grace through faith and as a gift from God, not the result of our works – but only as a result of God's work – it's speaking about salvation from the judgement our sins deserve, which is the second death in the lake of fire (Revelation 21:8). Now we move on to a second aspect of our salvation as we come to ...

Salvation from Sin's Power (Phil.2:12)

This is day by day salvation, requiring our action in co-operating with the work of the Holy Spirit within us. Our old self, or sinful nature, remains and so we still sin (1 John 1:8 shows us sinless perfection in our lives here as Christians is not possible). How thankful we are that we have an Advocate in Jesus (1 John 2:1) to plead our case! Sin's power is greater than us, but we have an Advocate (one who pleads for us) who is in God's presence and his power is much greater still. That's how it's possible for us to live as imitators of Christ (1 John 2:6).

1 Corinthians 10:12,13 tells us that we have no need to fail in any given situation, but if we do there remains the provision of 1 John 1:7-9. It's in the context of this daily struggle that the text in Philippians 2 is relevant: "So then ... just as you have always obeyed, not as in my presence only, but now much more in my absence, work out your salvation with fear and trembling; for it is God who is at work in you, both to will and to work for *His* good pleasure" (Philippians 2:12-13).

There in verse 12, Paul writes about our need to work out our own salvation day by day, referring to something requiring our co-operation with the work of the Holy Spirit within us. This is talking about a different aspect of our salvation: about being saved from the power of sin in our daily life as Christians. We can know salvation from the daily power of sin by confessing our known sins to God (1 John 1:7-9). And now lastly, let's turn to ...

Salvation from Sin's Presence (Rom.13:11)

This will take place at Christ's return for his Church when we are taken from this sinful world, and our bodies are made new and sinless (1 Thessalonians 4:13-18). This topic brings us to Romans chapter 13: *"Love does no wrong to a neighbor; therefore love is the fulfillment of the law. Do this, knowing the time, that it is already the hour for you to awaken from sleep; for now salvation is nearer to us than when we believed. The night is almost gone, and the day is near. Therefore let us lay aside the deeds of darkness and put on the armor of light. Let us behave properly as in the day ..."* (Romans 13:10-13).

That's the third aspect of salvation mentioned there in Romans 13:11. And it's a future aspect: because it's said to be now nearer to us than when we first believed. This is salvation from the very presence of sin, and it's to take place at Christ's return when he returns to take all Christian believers away from this sinful world. At that time in the future, our bodies will be made new (1 Thessalonians 4:13-18), never again to be capable of sinning.

It should now be clear that there really is an aspect of salvation which we can lose, and which is conditional – and that's salvation from the power of sin. This insight brings harmony to our understanding of God's Word concerning our salvation. Sadly, by not taking care to distinguish between these three aspects of salvation, some have wrongly taught that the believer's salvation from the penalty of his or her sin isn't secure or is a mixture of faith and works. Not so. God's promise to whoever believes in Jesus is eternal life (John 3:16; Romans 6:23). It's God's free gift to the believer.

And the main support for that is that the Bible teaches us that the primary salvation decision is God's, not ours - which means that any view which permits us to lose our salvation seriously underplays God's sovereignty. Jesus invited people to come to him and to rest in the knowledge of sins forgiven (Matthew 11:28). In itself that famous invitation at the end of Matthew chapter 11 invites people to stop relying on their own efforts to obtain salvation, and simply come and rest in the salvation which Christ is offering as a gift. But in John chapter 6, the Lord pulls back the curtain and reveals something of the bigger picture of what's involved in a sinner coming to Christ. He said in verse 37:

"All that the Father gives me will come to me, and whoever comes to me I will never cast out. For I have come down from heaven, not to do my own will but the will of him who sent me. And this is the will of him who sent me, that I should lose nothing of all that he has given me, but raise it up on the last day. For this is the will of my Father, that everyone who looks on the Son and believes in him should have eternal life, and I will raise him up on

the last day." ... *No one can come to me unless the Father who sent me draws him"* (John 6:44).

When we believe, it's as if Christ's death becomes our death and it's then that we receive new life in Christ. We're guaranteed never to face God's judgment for our sins simply because Jesus Christ served our sentence when dying on the cross. God reckoned that we were crucified with Christ when he died under our sentence of death, so it's all over and done with. And, of course, this covers all our sins in the future as well as our past sins as far as we're concerned. God doesn't make the same distinction between past and present as we do. He sees the end from the beginning. The whole landscape of time is always before God. God doesn't want us to remain blind to the security we have in our guaranteed salvation.

If you're someone who struggles with this teaching of the believer's eternal security in Christ, may I gently urge you to meditate on the Bible's presentation regarding our union with Christ? This lies at the root of any difficulty we may have in seeing our salvation as being for ever assured through Christ's death. If you struggle with that, might I suggest you've not yet seen clearly enough this amazing spiritual reality of our union with Christ? And it's truly amazing!

The words of John 14:20 are stunning. Here's what that verse says: "*On that day you will know that I am in My Father, and you are in Me, and I in you.*" Jesus has been saying quite repeatedly that he's in the Father and the Father is in him. That's the union of the Son with the Father (see also 10:38; 14:10,11; see 17:21). But then he adds that we are in him and he is in each of us. Take time to absorb that. Each of us is one with Christ – and this is being said in the same way that Jesus is one with the Father! That's why I say again that if you struggle with the idea of the believer's eternal security in Christ, may I ask you to meditate on this amazing spiritual reality of our union with Christ?

Later, in water baptism we demonstrate the fact of our union with Christ by 'acting it out' – i.e, being buried in water and rising up from it again. Water baptism is only a symbolic witness to all who watch it taking place that we're testifying to the faith that's already saved us – so our water baptism is in effect a drama about our previous identification, and prior involvement, with a crucified and resurrected saviour. We say again: Paul reasons that, if Christ died to sin, and we're identified with Christ, then it follows that we, too, died to sin – and as a practical consequence it would be inappropriate for us to lead a life dominated by sinful practices now. This is Paul's answer to critics who were saying that if a Christian believer has had all of his or her sins forgiven then why shouldn't they live as they please. Paul says the true preaching of salvation should never be misconstrued as a licence to keep on sinning.

And so we conclude our series of studies back where we began at Romans chapters 6 through 8. These chapters teach us that it can only be our blindness to the full glory of God's eternal purpose for us to be one with Christ that stops us from seeing our salvation as being for ever assured through Christ's death, once we have repented and placed genuine saving faith in the Lord Jesus – a real faith that motivates us to live a holy life for his glory, until he returns.

About Hayes Press

Hayes Press (www.hayespress.org) is a registered charity in the United Kingdom, whose primary mission is to disseminate the Word of God, mainly through literature. It is one of the largest distributors of gospel tracts and leaflets in the United Kingdom, with over 100 titles and many thousands dispatched annually. In addition to paperbacks and eBooks, Hayes Press also publishes Plus Eagles' Wings, a fun and educational Bible magazine for children, and Golden Bells, a popular daily Bible reading calendar in wall or desk formats.

If you would like to contact Hayes Press, there are a number of ways you can do so:

By mail: c/o The Barn, Flaxlands, Royal Wootton Bassett, Wiltshire, UK SN4 8DY

By phone: 01793 850598

By eMail: info@hayespress.org

via Facebook: www.facebook.com/hayespress.org

About the Author

Born and educated in Scotland, Brian worked as a government scientist until God called him into full-time Christian ministry on behalf of the Churches of God (www.churchesofgod.info). His voice has been heard on Search For Truth radio broadcasts for over 30 years (visit www.searchfortruth.podbean.com) during which time he has been an itinerant Bible teacher throughout the UK. His evangelical and missionary work outside the UK is primarily in Belgium, The Philippines and South East Central Africa. He is married to Rosemary, with a son and daughter.

Also by Brian Johnston

ONCE SAVED, ALWAYS SAVED? THE REALITY OF ETERNAL SECURITY

The issue of whether a "born-again" Christian can lose their salvation is an absolutely critical one and has been a controversial topic amongst Christians for centuries. Brian provides a number of faith lessons which include insightful illustrations and Biblical references that all Christians can use to reassure themselves that there is no basis in the Bible for the so-called "Falling Away Doctrine."

GET REAL: LIVING EVERY DAY AS AN AUTHENTIC FOLLOWER OF CHRIST

Do you ever feel like you're just playing at being a Christian? Perhaps you even feel a bit of a fake or even a hypocrite - but you don't know what to change or how to change it. Here is some helpful, practical and scriptural guidance on Bible study, personal and collective prayer, worship, church life and family life, with the goal of us becoming authentic, credible disciples who live with real integrity!

Deepening Our Relationship with Christ

The first step in our relationship with Jesus is accepting Him as our Saviour - but that's just the beginning! In this short book, Brian Johnston expounds 8 important ways that every Christian should deepen their personal relationship with Christ: (1) In being in union with Him, (2) In being built on Him, (3) In being United by and with Him, (4) In following Him, (5) In owning Him as Head of the Body, (6) In being added alongside Him, (7) In being subject to Him as Son over God's House, (8) In remembering Him.

www.ingramcontent.com/pod-product-compliance
Lightning Source LLC
Chambersburg PA
CBHW070314160726
47999CB00003B/1023